A Big Night at Maria's Café

Sheila Fletcher
Illustrated by Paul Gibbs

OXFORD
UNIVERSITY PRESS

198 Madison Avenue
New York, NY 10016 USA

Great Clarendon Street, Oxford ox2 6DP UK

Oxford University Press is a department of the University of Oxford. It furthers the University's objective of excellence in research, scholarship, and education by publishing worldwide in

Oxford   New York
Auckland Cape Town Dar es Salaam
Hong Kong Karachi Kuala Lumpur Madrid
Melbourne Mexico City Nairobi New Delhi
Shanghai Taipei Toronto

With offices in
Argentina Austria Brazil Chile Czech Republic
France Greece Guatemala Hungary Italy Japan
Poland Portugal Singapore South Korea
Switzerland Thailand Turkey Ukraine Vietnam

OXFORD and OXFORD ENGLISH are registered trademarks of Oxford University Press.

Photocopying

The Publisher grants permission for the photocopying of those pages marked "photocopiable" according to the following conditions. Individual purchasers may make copies for their own use or for use by classes that they teach. School purchasers may make copies for use by staff and students, but this permission does not extend to additional schools or branches.

Under no circumstances may any part of this book be photocopied for resale.

Any websites referred to in this publication are in the public domain and their addresses are provided by Oxford University Press for information only. Oxford University Press disclaims any responsibility for the content.

Executive Publishing Manager: Stephanie Karras
Managing Editor: Sharon Sargent
Design Manager: Stacy Merlin
Project Coordinator: Sarah Dentry
Production Layout Artist: Colleen Ho
Cover Design: Colleen Ho, Stacy Merlin, Michael Steinhofer
Manufacturing Manager: Shanta Persaud
Manufacturing Controller: Eve Wong

ISBN: 978 0 19474033 3 (BOOK)

ISBN: 978 0 19474039 5 (OPD READING LIBRARY)

ISBN: 978 0 19474056 2 (WORKPLACE READING LIBRARY)

Printed in China

10 9 8 7 6 5 4 3

This book is printed on paper from certified and well-managed sources.

Many thanks to Pronk&Associates, Kelly Stern, and Meg Brooks for a job well done.

A Big Night at Maria's Café

Table of Contents

A. Match the pictures with the words.

_g_ **1.** busser	___ **5.** hostess	___ **9.** server
___ **2.** chef	___ **6.** kitchen	___ **10.** staff
___ **3.** diner	___ **7.** menu	
___ **4.** dishwasher	___ **8.** place setting	

B. Answer the questions.

1. What kind of food do you like?
2. What's your favorite restaurant?
3. What do you like best about restaurants?
4. Which restaurant jobs are difficult?

C. Read the chapter titles of this book. Look at the pictures in the book. Then guess the answers to the questions. Circle *yes* or *no*.

1. Does this story happen in a restaurant?   yes   no

2. Did the restaurant hire a bad chef?   yes   no

3. Is the staff working hard?   yes   no

Chapter 1

A Special Dinner

Maria's Café is having a special dinner tonight. Maria and the staff want to help end hunger in their city. Sandra is a reporter. She's going to write an article about the dinner.

Maria: Good evening, Sandra. This is Emiko Osaka. She's the hostess tonight.

Sandra: It's nice to meet you, Emiko. Please tell me about the dinner.

Emiko: A lot of people are coming to Maria's Café tonight! The money is going to help hungry people in our city.

Sandra: What's the hostess's job tonight, Emiko?

Emiko: I greet the diners. Then I bring them to their table and tell them their server's name. I also give the diners their menus.

Sandra: Do you like your job?

Emiko: Well, tonight is my first night! But I like meeting new people. And Maria's Café is a great restaurant.

Sandra: I'm sure you're very excited!

Emiko: I am excited! I just hope I do a good job.

Sandra: Who's coming to the dinner tonight?

Emiko: Many important people. Mayor Adams is going to be here.

Sandra: How many people did Maria invite?

Emiko: About 100, I think. The dining room is going to be full tonight!

Sandra: How much does the dinner cost?

Emiko: Each person is paying $50. That's because it's a special event.

Sandra: So, I know you work hard in the dining room. What's happening in the kitchen?

Emiko: Yes, we work hard in the dining room, but the food is the most important thing. We have a great chef. Chef Ryan is the best! I'm going to take you to the kitchen. You can ask him about his job.

Sandra: Thank you! I'm sure cooking for an event like this is challenging.

A. Mark the sentences T (true) or F (false).

_T_ 1. The restaurant is having a dinner to help end hunger.

___ 2. Sandra is writing about the dinner.

___ 3. This is Emiko's last night at Maria's Café.

___ 4. Each person is paying $100 for the dinner.

___ 5. Sandra doesn't want to talk to Chef Ryan.

B. Complete the chart. Use the words in the box.

| ~~chef~~ | dining room | kitchen |
| menu | staff | table |

Rooms in a Restaurant	People in a Restaurant	Things Used in a Restaurant
	chef	

Complete the sentences. Use the words in the box.

| diner | hostess | reporter | ~~restaurant~~ | server |

1. The ____restaurant____ opens at 5:00 for dinner.

2. A _____ eats meals in a restaurant.

3. A _____ brings food to the tables.

4. The _____ brings diners to their tables.

5. A _____ writes stories about events.

C. Understand the main idea and details. Check (✔) the two details from the story that support this idea.

There is a special dinner at Maria's Café tonight.

_____ **a.** Many people are coming to Maria's tonight.

_____ **b.** The chef's name is Ryan.

_____ **c.** The money is going to help end hunger in the community.

_____ **d.** Emiko takes Sandra to the kitchen.

_____ **e.** It's Emiko's first night as a hostess.

What's Next in Chapter 2?

What's going to happen next? What do you think? Read the question. Then circle your guess, *yes* or *no*.

1. Is Sandra going to eat dinner at the restaurant?

   yes   no

2. Is Sandra going to help Chef Ryan?

   yes   no

3. Is Chef Ryan going to talk about problems in the kitchen?

   yes   no

Chapter 2

A Great Chef

Emiko: Chef Ryan, this is Sandra Watson. She's a reporter. She's writing a story about the dinner tonight. See you later, Sandra.

Sandra: It's good to meet you, Chef Ryan. How do you prepare for an event like this?

Chef Ryan: Well, first I have to hire extra workers for the kitchen. Then I plan the menu. I have to buy all the food, too. We need a lot of food for all these people!

Maria's Café

Menu for August 1st
"Help Us End Hunger"

Soup or Salad
Choose from tomato basil soup or a fresh garden salad.

Chicken, Fish, or Steak
Chicken and fish can be grilled or fried. Steak is served fresh from the grill.
Dinners come with vegetables and potatoes or rice.

Chocolate Cake with Strawberries or a Bowl of Mixed Berries
Tea, Coffee, or Soda

Sandra: What's on the menu tonight?

Chef Ryan: We have a special menu. First, diners can have soup or salad. Then they choose chicken, fish, or steak. Every dinner comes with vegetables and potatoes or rice.

Sandra: What about dessert?

Chef Ryan: For dessert, people can have chocolate cake with strawberries or a bowl of mixed berries. We're also serving tea, coffee, or soda.

Sandra: Mmm! That sounds good. I'm going to have the chocolate cake!

Sandra: This dinner is a lot of work for the staff.

Chef Ryan: Yes, it is, but I have a good team in the kitchen. Every job is important.

Sandra: Are there any special problems tonight?

Chef Ryan: Well, we have extra workers. So a lot of people are working in a small space. We need to work very quickly, too. We're going to serve 100 people at the same time!

Chef Ryan: Oops! There goes an egg! Kwan, our dishwasher, can clean that up. We need to clean up messes quickly. That keeps the kitchen safe. Every worker is important for tonight.

Sandra: Why is tonight important?

Chef Ryan: The event is going to make a lot of money. That's going to help hungry people. Also, this is a new restaurant. We want people to try our food and tell their friends.

Sandra: Good luck!

A. Circle the correct answer.

1. How does Chef Ryan prepare for the dinner?
   a. He hires extra workers.
   b. He cleans the refrigerator.

2. What's different about the dinner tonight?
   a. There's a special menu.
   b. The chef is serving dessert.

3. What is one problem in the kitchen today?
   a. The chef can't buy the food.
   b. There are a lot of people in the kitchen.

B. Label the pictures. Use the words in the box.

| chocolate cake | ~~egg~~ | mess | reporter | steak | team |

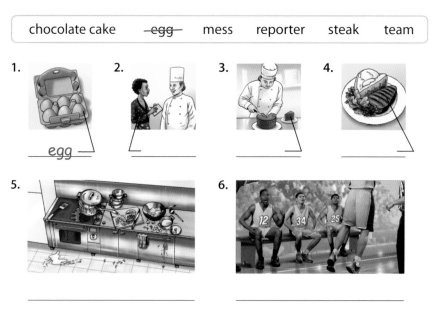

1. _egg_

2. _____

3. _____

4. _____

5. _____

6. _____

C. Understand the main idea and details.

1. *The kitchen at Maria's is a very busy place tonight.*
   Check (✔) the two details from the story that
   support this idea.

   ____ **a.** There are extra workers in the kitchen.

   ____ **b.** Diners can have mixed berries for dessert.

   ____ **c.** Kwan is a dishwasher.

   ____ **d.** The chef is preparing food for 100 people.

   ____ **e.** Sandra's going to have the chocolate cake.

2. Which food is not on the menu?
   a. spaghetti
   b. chicken, fish, or steak
   c. chocolate cake or a bowl of berries

3. How does Chef Ryan need to keep the kitchen?
   a. dirty
   b. safe
   c. quiet

What's Next in Chapter 3?

**What's going to happen next? What do you think?
Circle or write your guess.**

What is Sandra going to do?
   a. eat chocolate cake
   b. talk to the rest of the staff
   c. write her story
   d. other: _____

Chapter 3

A Good Staff

Sandra: So, what's your job tonight, Kwan?

Kwan: I wash all the dishes and put them in the dish room. I clean up messes. The chef needs to keep the kitchen clean and safe. I help him.

Sandra: Do you like working at Maria's Café?

Kwan: Yes. Chef Ryan is great. I'm learning a lot from him. Maybe some day I can be a chef!

Sandra: Thanks, Kwan. I'm going to find out what the bussers are doing.

Sandra: Excuse me. Are you a busser?

Antonio: Yes, I'm Antonio.

Sandra: It's nice to meet you. I'm Sandra. What are you doing tonight?

Antonio: Now, I'm setting the tables. When people sit down, I'm going to take away extra place settings. I also take away dirty dishes and bring bread and butter to the tables.

Sandra: You're going to be busy! Do you know where I can find a server?

Antonio: Raul is over there.

Sandra: Hi, Raul. It's going to be a busy night for the servers!

Raul: Yes, it is. I have to take the orders and give them to Chef Ryan. Then I have to serve the food when it's ready. I need to watch my tables carefully. I want people to be happy with their dinner.

Sandra: Do you ever worry about dropping things?

Raul: No, I don't. I'm very good at my job.

Sandra: It's almost time for dinner! The guests are at the door. Is everything ready, Emiko?

Emiko: I think so. Each table has place settings and fresh flowers. Chef Ryan says that the food is ready. It's time to open the door and welcome the guests!

Sandra: Good luck!

Emiko: Thanks!

Maria: Mayor Adams, welcome to Maria's Café!

Emiko: Good evening, Mayor Adams. Your table is right over here. This is Raul. He's going to be your server tonight.

19

A. Mark the sentences T (true) or F (false). Change the false sentences. Make them true.

_F_ 1. Kwan doesn't like his job at Maria's.
   <u>Kwan likes his job at Maria's.</u>

____ 2. Kwan wants to be a chef some day.

____ 3. Antonio takes away extra place settings.

____ 4. Raul is worried about dropping things.

____ 5. The flowers and place settings aren't on the tables.

____ 6. Maria welcomes Mayor Adams to the restaurant.

B. Complete the sentences. Use the words in the box.

busser	careful	drop
guests	place setting	worry

1. The hostess welcomes the _____ at the door.

2. Don't _____ ! We're going to get there on time.

3. Servers should be _____ with hot dishes.

4. There is an extra diner at this table. We need another
   _____ .

5. The _____ takes away dirty dishes.

6. You're carrying too many glasses. You're going to
   _____ one.

C. Understand the main idea and details. Circle the correct answer.

1. What is this chapter about? Choose the main idea.
   a. how a restaurant makes money to help end hunger
   b. what a restaurant's staff is going to do during a dinner
   c. how to interview a restaurant's staff

2. Who brings the orders to the chef?
   a. the hostess
   b. the server
   c. the dishwasher

3. Who brings bread and butter to the table?
   a. the chef
   b. the server
   c. the busser

What's Next in Chapter 4?

What's going to happen next? What do you think? Circle or write your guess.

What's going to happen during the dinner?
   a. Raul is going to drop something.
   b. Maria is going to give the mayor a check.
   c. The diners are going to say, "This food is bad!"
   d. other: _____

Chapter 4

The Big Night!

Emiko: Welcome to Maria's Café! We're so glad you came tonight. Here's your table.

Mayor: Thank you! This is our first time eating here.

Emiko: Antonio, can you please remove the extra place settings at this table?

Antonio: Sure, no problem!

Emiko: Our chef has a special menu tonight. Oh dear, I forgot the menus!

Raul: Don't worry, Emiko. I have them right here.

Maria: I'm so excited that you're all here. I want to thank you for making this a special night. This dinner is going to help many people in our community. Mayor Adams, here is a check for $5,000!

Mayor Adams: Thank you for all of your hard work, Maria. The food and the service were excellent. You have a great staff! Maria's Café is going to be an important part of our community.

Emiko: The last guest is gone, and the doors are closed. I'm so tired. I think we did a great job!

Maria: This was a great night! The food was good, and everyone had a good time. We also made a lot of money to help end hunger in this city.

Chef Ryan: We work well as a team.

Maria: Thank you, everyone, for your help and hard work.

A Dinner to Help End Hunger

by Sandra Watson

Maria's Café had a big night last night. They had a special dinner. The money they made is going to help end hunger in our city.

Everyone at the café worked very hard. It was hostess Emiko Osaka's first night on the job, but she made the guests feel welcome. Chef Ryan had a special menu. The servers, bussers, and dishwashers all worked together.

About 100 people came to the dinner. The cost was $50 for each person. Café owner Maria Gonzales said, "We had a great dinner last night. Everyone had a good time and we made $5,000. This money is going to help hungry people in our community. We're all very happy!"

Mayor Adams thanked Maria and her staff for all their hard work. He said, "No one was hungry at Maria's Café tonight!"

Reading Check

A. These sentences are false. Make them true.

1. Raul welcomes the guests at the door.
   <u>Emiko welcomes the guests at the door.</u>
2. Maria gives Mayor Adams a check for $500.
3. The guests don't like the food.
4. Emiko isn't tired at the end of the night.
5. Sandra's article says that the staff didn't work together.

B. Circle the correct word.

1. That's Ana's café. Ana is the ((owner) / hostess).
2. A busser needs to keep the tables (safe / clean).
3. The mayor is an important (reporter / guest).
4. Restaurant workers need to work as a (team / manager).

C. Match the main idea of each chapter with a detail.

Main Ideas	Details
<u>d</u> 1. There's a special dinner at Maria's Café.	a. Raul takes care of the diners at his tables.
___ 2. Ryan is a great chef.	b. The restaurant makes a lot of money.
___ 3. The staff works hard.	c. He prepares a special menu.
___ 4. The event is a success.	d. Many important people are coming.

What's Next?

What's going to happen next? What do you think? Circle your guess, *yes* or *no*.

1. Is Chef Ryan going to open a restaurant?

   yes   no

2. Is Emiko going to keep working at Maria's Café?

   yes   no

3. Is Kwan going to work as a chef?

   yes   no

A. Read ads.

Book Sale...

When? Friday to Sunday
7:00 a.m. to 5:00 p.m. each day

Where? Plumwood Community Center
243 Plum Creek Circle

Why? to buy new equipment for the community playground

- Read the book sale ad above.
- Look for ads in the newspaper or on the Internet. Look for events that are going to help the community.
- Read the ads. What is for sale? Who is the money going to help?

B. Write an ad.

- Think about your community. Who needs help? Does a school need new equipment? Does the community center need new toys or books?

- Write an ad for an event to make money for your community. Be sure to say when, where, and why.

- Share your ad with your class.

Useful Expressions

When is the event?

Where is the event?

Why are you having the event?

Shared vocabulary from the *OPD*
and *A Big Night at Maria's Café*

busser
[bŭ**/**sər]

chef
[shĕf]

city
[sĭt**/**ē]

diner
[dīn**/**ər]

dining room
[dī**/**nĭng rōōm**/**]

dishwasher
[dĭsh**/**wä**/**shər]

hostess
[hō**/**stəs]

hungry
[hŭng**/**grē]

kitchen
[kĭch**/**ən]

OPD Link

menu
[měn/yōō]

mess
[měs]

place setting
[plās/ sět/ĭng]

reporter
[rĭ pör/tər]

server
[sür/vər]

staff
[stăf]

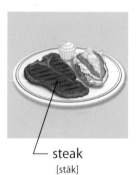

steak
[stāk]

take the order
[tāk/ dhē ör/dər]

team
[tēm]